THE 12 NAMES OF GOD

PRAYER JOURNAL 2006

THE 12 NAMES OF GOD

PRAYER JOURNAL

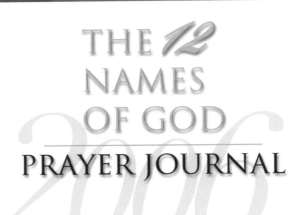

Dear Friend,

Prayer is a powerful weapon.

Prayer produces results and unleashes supernatural power for victory.

Prayer is a force that crosses the borders of time and invites the eternal power of God into your life and the lives of your loved ones!

In the words of the great Bible teacher E. M. Bounds, "Our praying needs to be pressed and pursued with an energy that never tires, a persistency which will not be denied, and a courage which never fails."

This journal has been written to help you become even more faithful and persistent in your prayers during the coming year. And as you pray, the study of God's names each month is provided to help you know Him in a deeper way than you've ever imagined.

Features of this journal include:

- In-depth teaching on the twelve revelations of God's name—from *Elohim* (My Creator) throughout the month of January to *Jehovah Shammah* (My Abiding Presence) during December.

- Monthly Prayer Points that allow you to join ministry friends and intercessors around the world, strategically agreeing in prayer on crusades, events, and outreaches touching our world.

- Scripture passages throughout the year to inspire and empower you to live the abundant life in Christ Jesus.

- The opportunity to chronicle your walk with God and to be enriched as you revisit the life lessons you have recorded during the year.

Man's chief end and ultimate purpose is to know God, and this occurs through an unfolding revelation of who He truly is, for John 17:3 declares: *"And this is life eternal; that they might know thee, the only true God."* In grasping a deeper dimension of who God is through each revelation of His name, we begin to discover the ultimate purpose for which we exist—to know our magnificent, unfathomable, mighty God in all His power and glory forever and ever.

That is my prayer for you, for as your understanding of God deepens, you can pray with greater effectiveness and results. When you pray as our Lord Jesus taught, *"Our Father"* and *"Hallowed be thy name"* (Matthew 6:9), you sanctify His holy name. You honor and glorify His blessed name.

Your prayer life will be changed forever as you discover how the name of the Lord is revealed throughout His Word. May you approach His presence with a growing, deepening love and reverence throughout the coming year. And day by day, may you learn what it means to call Him My Elohim, My Jehovah, My El Shaddai, My Adonai, My Jehovah Jireh, My Jehovah Rophe, My Jehovah Nissi, My Jehovah Mikkadesh, My Jehovah Tsidkenu, My Jehovah Shalom, My Jehovah Rohi, and My Jehovah Shammah.

May this journal help you take the journey of a lifetime!

For the glory of our wonderful Lord Jesus...

Everlastingly at it,

Benny Hinn

Elohim

"THE NAME *ELOHIM* IS ALWAYS CONNECTED TO CREATION AND POWER. STRONG FAITH AND EFFECTIVE PRAYER IS BASED UPON A TRUE REVELATION OF GOD'S CREATIVE POWER. WE RECOGNIZE GOD'S AUTHORITY AND DOMINION OVER US IN PRAYER, ACKNOWLEDGING HE IS GOD, OUR CREATOR."

—BENNY HINN

My Creator

ELOHIM

Elohim—"Creator"—is used 2,570 times in the Old Testament. It is the Hebrew word for God used most often, first in Genesis 1:1: *"In the beginning **God** created the heaven and the earth."* God was the Creator—the Creator of everything—long before He was our Father.

The name Elohim is always connected to creation and power. In Exodus 3:4, the voice of Elohim spoke from the midst of a bush, calling Moses to lead the children of Israel from captivity. In Exodus 20:3, God commanded His children to have no other gods before Him.

Throughout the Bible, the name of God is more than a distinguishing title. The name represents God's divine nature and relationship to His people. The various names of God represent Him as He is known, and through the name Elohim, He presents Himself—His love, power, mercy, and glory—to His creation.

True prayer is impossible without the knowledge of God Almighty as our Creator.

Benny Hinn

JANUARY

S	M	T	W	T	F	S
1	2	3	4	5	6	7
8	9	10	11	12	13	14
15	16	17	18	19	20	21
22	23	24	25	26	27	28
29	30	31				

ELOHIM

_____

_____

_____

_____

_____

_____

_____

_____

_____

_____

_____

_____

_____

_____

ELOHIM

My Creator

"And God said, Let there be light: and there was light.... And God said, Let there be a firmament in the midst of the waters, and let it divide the waters from the waters.... And God said, Let the waters under the heaven be gathered together unto one place, and let the dry land appear: and it was so."

—Genesis 1:3, 6, 9

Only the Holy Spirit can reveal our Creator to our hearts. This takes place at salvation.

Benny Hinn

ELOHIM

JANUARY

S	M	T	W	T	F	S
1	2	3	4	5	6	7
8	9	10	11	12	13	14
15	16	17	18	19	20	21
22	23	24	25	26	27	28
29	30	31				

_____

_____

_____

_____

_____

_____

_____

_____

_____

_____

_____

_____

_____

_____

_____

_____

_____

_____

E L O H I M

My Creator

"I am the LORD thy God, which have brought thee out of the land of
Egypt, out of the house of bondage."

—Exodus 20:2

ELOHIM

JANUARY

S	M	T	W	T	F	S
1	2	3	4	5	6	7
8	9	10	11	12	13	14
15	16	17	18	19	20	21
22	23	24	25	26	27	28
29	30	31				

At the moment of salvation, the Holy Spirit reveals God's omnipotence, God's omniscience, and God's omnipresence, the One who is all-powerful, all-knowing, and rules all—God Almighty.

Benny Hinn

_____

_____

_____

_____

_____

_____

_____

_____

_____

_____

_____

_____

_____

ELOHIM
My Creator

"Paul, a servant of Jesus Christ, called to be an apostle, separated unto the gospel of God, (Which he had promised afore by his prophets in the holy scriptures,) Concerning his Son Jesus Christ our Lord, which was made of the seed of David according to the flesh; And declared to be the Son of God with power, according to the spirit of holiness, by the resurrection from the dead."

—Romans 1:1-4

When we come to God, we sanctify His holy name. Effective prayer is impossible unless we stand in awe at the mention of His name.

Benny Hinn

ELOHIM

JANUARY

S	M	T	W	T	F	S
1	2	3	4	5	6	7
8	9	10	11	12	13	14
15	16	17	18	19	20	21
22	23	24	25	26	27	28
29	30	31				

_____

_____

_____

_____

_____

_____

_____

_____

_____

_____

_____

_____

_____

E L O H I M
My Creator

"Blessed be the God and Father of our Lord Jesus Christ, which according to his abundant mercy hath begotten us again unto a lively hope by the resurrection of Jesus Christ from the dead, To an inheritance incorruptible, and undefiled, and that fadeth not away, reserved in heaven for you, Who are kept by the power of God through faith unto salvation ready to be revealed in the last time."

—1 Peter 1:3-5

Jehovah

"THE NAME JEHOVAH IS REVEALED IN CONNECTION WITH THE CREATION OF ADAM AND DEALS WITH GOD'S COVENANT WITH HIS PEOPLE."

—BENNY HINN

JEHOVAH

My Lord God

Jehovah or *Yahweh* — "my Lord God" — occurs 6,823 times in the Old Testament. An example is in Genesis 2:7: *"And the LORD God formed man of the dust of the ground, and breathed into his nostrils the breath of life; and man became a living soul."* The name Jehovah is revealed in connection with the creation of Adam and deals with God's covenant with His people, and it is also used throughout the Old Testament in connection with God's covenants with the children of Israel.

While the name Elohim presents God, we see His personality revealed in Jehovah, for it is connected to covenant, relationship, fellowship, and blood sacrifice. Elohim presents love, while Jehovah reveals love. Elohim presents power, yet Jehovah reveals His power. Elohim presents mercy, and Jehovah reveals mercy. In Elohim, God presents His glory, yet through Jehovah He reveals His glory.

He is a covenant-keeping God who will never leave us, fail us, or forsake us. Glory to the name Jehovah!

Prayer Points:

- Join in prayer for God's power to be poured out in Louisiana during the February 2–3, 2006, Holy Spirit Miracle Crusade in Baton Rouge (the River Center Arena).

- Agree for Benny Hinn Ministries Spanish-language telecasts to continue to expand throughout the Americas. Also pray for our 24-hour-a-day Arabic-language satellite network that blankets the Middle East, Europe, and North Africa with teaching, preaching, and original dramatic programs.

- Pastor Benny's desire to reach young people around the world continues to expand through explosive youth services that continue to fill the largest arenas. Pray for God's power to be poured out on teenagers and young adults who in turn can help reach the world for the Savior.

- Agree in prayer that our www.BennyHinn.org Web site will continue to be used mightily as an exciting, powerful tool for spreading the Gospel and sharing what God is doing through this ministry.

God's personality is revealed as Jehovah through covenant, relationship, fellowship, and blood sacrifice.

Benny Hinn

JEHOVAH

FEBRUARY

S	M	T	W	T	F	S
29	30	31	1	2	3	4
5	6	7	8	9	10	11
12	13	14	15	16	17	18
19	20	21	22	23	24	25
26	27	28				

_____

_____

_____

_____

_____

_____

_____

_____

_____

_____

_____

_____

JEHOVAH
My Lord God

"Behold, I will send my messenger, and he shall prepare the way before me: and the LORD, whom ye seek, shall suddenly come to his temple, even the messenger of the covenant, whom ye delight in: behold, he shall come, saith the LORD of hosts [Jehovah]."

—Malachi 3:1

Many individuals today only know God as Elohim. They have never met Jehovah or experienced a revelation of who He is through a covenant relationship.

Benny Hinn

JEHOVAH

FEBRUARY

S	M	T	W	T	F	S
			1	2	3	4
5	6	7	8	9	10	11
12	13	14	15	16	17	18
19	20	21	22	23	24	25
26	27	28				

_____

_____

_____

_____

_____

_____

_____

_____

_____

_____

_____

_____

_____

_____

_____

_____

_____

JEHOVAH

My Lord God

"And I appeared unto Abraham, unto Isaac, and unto Jacob, by the name of God Almighty, but by my name JEHOVAH was I not known to them."

—Exodus 6:3

Because of the life, death, and resurrection of Jesus Christ, believers can experience a covenant relationship and intimate fellowship with Jehovah.   *Benny Hinn*

JEHOVAH

FEBRUARY

S	M	T	W	T	F	S
			1	2	3	4
5	6	7	8	9	10	11
12	13	14	15	16	17	18
19	20	21	22	23	24	25
26	27	28				

_____

_____

_____

_____

_____

_____

_____

_____

_____

_____

_____

_____

_____

_____

_____

_____

_____

JEHOVAH
My Lord God

"That men may know that thou, whose name alone is JEHOVAH, art the most high over all the earth."

—Psalm 83:18

Strong, effective, and fervent prayer begins when the Holy Spirit reveals God Almighty as Jehovah.

Benny Hinn

JEHOVAH

FEBRUARY

S	M	T	W	T	F	S
			1	2	3	4
5	6	7	8	9	10	11
12	13	14	15	16	17	18
19	20	21	22	23	24	25
26	27	28				

_____

_____

_____

_____

_____

_____

_____

_____

_____

_____

_____

_____

_____

_____

_____

_____

_____

JEHOVAH
My Lord God

"Trust ye in the LORD for ever: for in the LORD JEHOVAH is everlasting strength."

—Isaiah 26:4

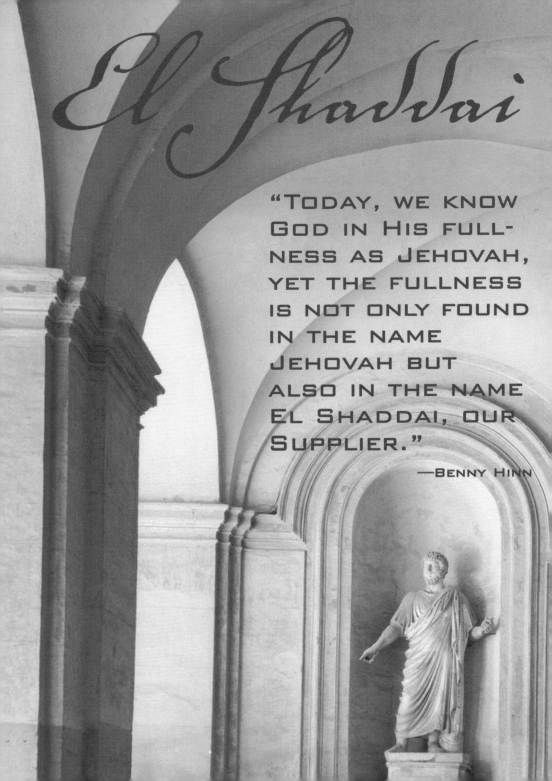

El Shaddai

"TODAY, WE KNOW GOD IN HIS FULL-NESS AS JEHOVAH, YET THE FULLNESS IS NOT ONLY FOUND IN THE NAME JEHOVAH BUT ALSO IN THE NAME EL SHADDAI, OUR SUPPLIER."

—BENNY HINN

My Supplier

E L   S H A D D A I

El Shaddai—"God Almighty, my Supply, my Nourishment"—the third name of God, used seven times in the Old Testament, was revealed to Abraham, called Abram at that time: *"And when Abram was ninety years old and nine, the LORD appeared to Abram, and said unto him, I am the Almighty God [El Shaddai]; walk before me, and be thou perfect. And I will make my covenant between me and thee, and will multiply thee exceedingly"* (Genesis 17:1).

At the age of 99, with his wife's womb barren, it would seem that God's promise that Abram's seed would inherit the land would have been impossible to fulfill. Yet he experienced a revelation of El Shaddai as God's promise was fulfilled through the birth of his son Isaac. The seed came after the revelation of El Shaddai: the Supplier, the Nourisher, the all-sufficient One.

God made a covenant with Abram the moment he received the revelation, saying: *"Neither shall thy name any more be called Abram, but thy name shall be Abraham; for a father of many nations have I made thee. And I will make thee exceeding fruitful, and I will make nations of thee, and kings shall come out of thee"* (Genesis 17:5-6).

Today, we know God in His fullness as Jehovah, yet the fullness is not only found in the name Jehovah but also in the name El Shaddai, our Supplier. He is everything we could possibly need, exactly when we need it.

El Shaddai supplies everything we could possibly need, exactly when we need it.

Benny Hinn

EL SHADDAI

MARCH

S	M	T	W	T	F	S
26	27	28	1	2	3	4
5	6	7	8	9	10	11
12	13	14	15	16	17	18
19	20	21	22	23	24	25
26	27	28	29	30	31	

_____

_____

_____

_____

_____

_____

_____

_____

_____

_____

_____

_____

_____

_____

E L   S H A D D A I
My Supplier

"Even by the God of thy father, who shall help thee; and by the Almighty, who shall bless thee with blessings of heaven above, blessings of the deep that lieth under, blessings of the breasts, and of the womb."

—Genesis 49:25

Nothing is too difficult for El Shaddai, our Supplier! Our weakness is made strong through Him.

Benny Hinn

EL SHADDAI

MARCH

S	M	T	W	T	F	S
			1	2	3	4
5	6	7	8	9	10	11
12	13	14	15	16	17	18
19	20	21	22	23	24	25
26	27	28	29	30	31	

EL SHADDAI

My Supplier

"And thou shalt know that I the LORD am thy Saviour and thy Redeemer, the mighty One of Jacob."

—Isaiah 60:16

MARCH 12–18

The Word of God teaches us that El Shaddai knows our needs intimately, yet we receive nothing until we ask.

Benny Hinn

EL SHADDAI

MARCH

S	M	T	W	T	F	S
			1	2	3	4
5	6	7	8	9	10	11
12	13	14	15	16	17	18
19	20	21	22	23	24	25
26	27	28	29	30	31	

_____

_____

_____

_____

_____

_____

_____

_____

_____

_____

_____

_____

_____

_____

_____

_____

_____

_____

_____

EL SHADDAI

My Supplier

"The Spirit of God hath made me, and the breath of the Almighty hath given me life."

—Job 33:4

By asking specifically and in faith, you acknowledge your dependence upon El Shaddai continually.

Benny Hinn

EL SHADDAI

MARCH

S	M	T	W	T	F	S
			1	2	3	4
5	6	7	8	9	10	11
12	13	14	15	16	17	18
19	20	21	22	23	24	25
26	27	28	29	30	31	

_____

_____

_____

_____

_____

_____

_____

_____

_____

_____

_____

_____

_____

_____

_____

_____

_____

EL SHADDAI

My Supplier

"He that dwelleth in the secret place of the most High shall abide under the shadow of the Almighty."

—Psalm 91:1

Adonai

"GOD REVEALS HIS WILL TO THOSE WHO KNOW HIM AS ADONAI—MASTER AND LORD."

—BENNY HINN

My Master

A D O N A I

Prayer Points:

- Lift up the untold millions who have experienced God's saving and healing touch through powerful demonstrations through Holy Spirit Miracle Crusades around the globe, including the largest healing services ever recorded in history.

- Agree in prayer for a powerful outpouring of God's power during the April 14 Good Friday Service in Dallas, Texas (American Airlines Arena).

- Each day we receive a million or more "hits" from Internet users around the world, including many regions where Christian activity is prohibited. Pray for God to use this effective method our ministry is utilizing to fulfill God's call to the "uttermost."

- Pray for a special anointing of God's saving and healing power during the Holy Spirit Miracle Crusade, April 28–30, 2006, in Copenhagen, Denmark.

Adonai—"Master and Lord"—is used in Genesis 18:2. When Abraham saw God coming in the noon of the day with two angels to destroy Sodom and Gomorrah, he ran to meet them before the tent door, bowed himself before them, and said, *"[Adonai!] My Lord, if now I have found favour in thy sight, pass not away, I pray thee, from thy servant"* (verse 3), and he became the great intercessor, for Scripture tells us, *"And Abraham drew near, and said, Wilt thou also destroy the righteous with the wicked?"* (verse 23).

God reveals His will to those who know Him as Adonai—Master and Lord. Up to this time Abraham did not have a full understanding of God's will. That is why he tried to help God accomplish the promise to make him the father of many nations when he took Hagar as a wife. The moment Abraham calls Him Adonai, Genesis 18:17 records: *"And the Lord said, Shall I hide from Abraham that thing which I do,"* referring to what God was about to do in Sodom. When Abraham addressed Him as Adonai, he was actually saying, "You are my Lord," and God responded by revealing His plan for Sodom.

Written 434 times in the Old Testament, this name indicates "mastership" and "ownership." Calling the Lord Adonai acknowledges His outright ownership over our lives totally, and when we call Him Adonai, we say to Him, "We are Your servants forever."

Addressing God as Adonai acknowledges God's absolute ownership of all we possess.

Benny Hinn

ADONAI

APRIL

S	M	T	W	T	F	S
26	27	28	29	30	31	1
2	3	4	5	6	7	8
9	10	11	12	13	14	15
16	17	18	19	20	21	22
23	24	25	26	27	28	29
30						

A D O N A I

My Master

"I will praise thee, O Lord my God, with all my heart: and I will glorify thy name for evermore."

—Psalm 86:12

APRIL 2–8

ADONAI

Great intercessors are born in intimate fellowship with God. As Abraham "drew near," he experienced intimacy with God Almighty and became a powerful intercessor.

Benny Hinn

APRIL

S	M	T	W	T	F	S
						1
2	3	4	5	6	7	8
9	10	11	12	13	14	15
16	17	18	19	20	21	22
23	24	25	26	27	28	29
30						

_____

_____

_____

_____

_____

_____

_____

_____

_____

_____

_____

_____

_____

_____

_____

_____

_____

A D O N A I
My Master

"Now know I that the LORD saveth his anointed; he will hear him
from his holy heaven with the saving strength of his right hand."

—Psalm 20:6

Adonai refers to God's true ownership of man. We are not our own. God alone has the right to direct our paths.

Benny Hinn

ADONAI

APRIL

S	M	T	W	T	F	S
						1
2	3	4	5	6	7	8
9	10	11	12	13	14	15
16	17	18	19	20	21	22
23	24	25	26	27	28	29
30						

_____

_____

_____

_____

_____

_____

_____

_____

_____

_____

_____

_____

_____

A D O N A I
My Master

"Some trust in chariots, and some in horses: but we will remember the name of the LORD our God. They are brought down and fallen: but we are risen, and stand upright. Save, LORD: let the king hear us when we call."

—Psalm 20:7-9

Adonai not only promises to guide our steps, but when we ask for His help, He will provide us with the ability to accomplish each task He gives us to do.

Benny Hinn

ADONAI

APRIL

S	M	T	W	T	F	S
						1
2	3	4	5	6	7	8
9	10	11	12	13	14	15
16	17	18	19	20	21	22
23	24	25	26	27	28	29
30						

_____

_____

_____

_____

_____

_____

_____

_____

_____

_____

_____

_____

_____

_____

_____

A D O N A I

My Master

"I will take the cup of salvation, and call upon the name of the Lord."

—Psalm 116:13

It is God's will that we ask for His guidance and protection. And as we do, He will lead us into a life of righteousness and into that place of refuge.

Benny Hinn

ADONAI

APRIL

S	M	T	W	T	F	S
						1
2	3	4	5	6	7	8
9	10	11	12	13	14	15
16	17	18	19	20	21	22
23	24	25	26	27	28	29
30						

_____

_____

_____

_____

_____

_____

_____

_____

_____

_____

_____

_____

_____

_____

_____

_____

_____

_____

_____

_____

ADONAI
My Master

"The LORD of hosts is with us; the God of Jacob is our refuge."

—Psalm 46:7

Jehovah Jireh

"And at that moment God revealed His Son's death on the cross to Abraham. The Lord Jesus said, 'Your father Abraham rejoiced to see my day: and he saw it, and was glad' (John 8:56)."

—Benny Hinn

My Provider

Prayer Points:

- Agree for a powerful outpouring during the Holy Spirit Miracle Crusade Service, May 12, 2006, in Billings, Montana (Metro Park Arena).

- Pray for our continued outreaches with assistance to victims of terrorist attacks, earthquakes, floods, tsunami-related tragedies, and hurricane destruction. Partners of Benny Hinn Ministries literally reach out in the midst of chaos and disaster with food, temporary shelter, and hope.

- Ask for a special anointing during the May 19–21 Holy Spirit Miracle Crusade in Trinidad/Tobago to touch a multitude of souls in this "true jewel of the Caribbean."

- Lift up ongoing Benny Hinn Ministries programs that help feed and care for tens of thousands of children and their families around the world every month! We continue to develop, build, open, and help operate centers for homeless children in such far-reaching, needy locations as Mexico, Bangladesh, Cambodia, India, Thailand, Russia, and the Philippines.

Jehovah Jireh—"the Lord my Provider" and "my Vision," or "the One I see"—occurs only once in the Old Testament (Genesis 22:14). In the ultimate act of obedience, Abraham took Isaac to Mount Moriah as God commanded to sacrifice his son.

And when Abraham approached the place where he was to build an altar, Isaac asked: *"Behold the fire and the wood: but where is the lamb for a burnt offering?"* (Genesis 22:7). Abraham told his son, *"God will provide himself a lamb for a burnt offering: so they went both of them together"* (verse 8). He bound his son to the altar, and as he stretched his hand to slay Isaac, the angel of the Lord stopped him: *"And he said, Lay not thine hand upon the lad, neither do thou any thing unto him: for now I know that thou fearest God, seeing thou hast not withheld thy son, thine only son from me"* (verse 12).

Abraham was shown a ram caught in a nearby thicket. When he looked and saw the sacrifice God had provided as a substitute for Isaac, he called the name of that place Jehovahjireh: *"And Abraham called the name of that place Jehovahjireh: as it is said to this day, In the mount of the LORD it shall be seen"* (verse 14).

And at that moment God revealed His Son's death on the cross to Abraham, for the Lord Jesus said, *"Your father Abraham rejoiced to see my day: and he saw it, and was glad"* (John 8:56).

APRIL 30–MAY 6

The revelation contained in Abraham's response is glorious! When Isaac asked, "Where is the lamb?" Abraham was actually saying, "Jehovah shall be seen!"

Benny Hinn

JEHOVAH JIREH

MAY

S	M	T	W	T	F	S
30	1	2	3	4	5	6
7	8	9	10	11	12	13
14	15	16	17	18	19	20
21	22	23	24	25	26	27
28	29	30	31			

JEHOVAH JIREH

My Provider

"Behold the fire and the wood: but where is the lamb for a burnt offering?"

—Genesis 22:7

The place where Isaac was offered (Mount Moriah) is the same place where Christ was crucified (Golgotha).

Benny Hinn

JEHOVAH JIREH

MAY

S	M	T	W	T	F	S
	1	2	3	4	5	6
7	8	9	10	11	12	13
14	15	16	17	18	19	20
21	22	23	24	25	26	27
28	29	30	31			

_____

_____

_____

_____

_____

_____

_____

_____

_____

_____

_____

_____

_____

_____

_____

_____

_____

_____

JEHOVAH JIREH

My Provider

"God will provide himself a lamb for a burnt offering."

—Genesis 22:8

In that moment Abraham was shown a vision of Christ on the cross.

Benny Hinn

MAY

S	M	T	W	T	F	S
	1	2	3	4	5	6
7	8	9	10	11	12	13
14	15	16	17	18	19	20
21	22	23	24	25	26	27
28	29	30	31			

JEHOVAH JIREH

JEHOVAH JIREH

My Provider

"And Abraham called the name of that place Jehovahjireh: as it is said to this day, In the mount of the LORD it shall be seen."

—Genesis 22:14

Provision is impossible without possession. Abraham's needs were supplied because he obeyed God's command.

Benny Hinn

JEHOVAH JIREH

MAY

S	M	T	W	T	F	S
	1	2	3	4	5	6
7	8	9	10	11	12	13
14	15	16	17	18	19	20
21	22	23	24	25	26	27
28	29	30	31			

Jehovah Rophe

"WHEN YOU SEE THE LAMB
AS YOUR PROVIDER, HEALING
COMES AS JEHOVAH ROPHE
IS REVEALED."

—BENNY HINN

My Healer

JEHOVAH ROPHE

Prayer Points:

- Lift up Pastor Benny and the crusade team as they minister during the massive June 10 youth service in the Minneapolis Target Center. Pray for an outpouring upon the youth to ignite a far-reaching revival.

- Pray for the millions of Web site visitors, who are now able to view live "streaming" Webcasts of *This Is Your Day!* and *Manna from Heaven*, receive information about Benny Hinn Ministries' activities, and access powerful resources in sections such as Religion in the News, Spiritual Life, Healing, Financial Freedom, Healthy Living, Family, Prophecy, and Salvation.

- Ask for a special anointing at the June 23–24, 2006, Holy Spirit Miracle Crusade in Sydney, Australia's Superdome. Pray for God's saving and miracle-working power to be poured out mightily.

- Agree in prayer for the operations of the Calcutta Mercy Hospital in India. Benny Hinn Ministries partners have helped support this vital medical outreach, and now the ministry completely underwrites all expenses of the hospital, where over 200,000 patients are treated each year.

Jehovah Rophe—"the Lord who heals"—is used only once in the Old Testament. In Exodus 15:26, the Lord made a healing covenant with the children of Israel after their deliverance from Egypt:

> *If thou wilt diligently hearken to the voice of the LORD thy God, and wilt do that which is right in his sight, and wilt give ear to his commandments, and keep all his statutes, I will put none of these diseases upon thee, which I have brought upon the Egyptians: for I am the LORD that healeth thee.*

Amazingly, these revelations appear in the Word of God in such perfect order under the inspiration of the Holy Spirit, for to know Him as Jehovah Rophe, your Healer, you must first know Him as your God, your Father, your Supplier, your Master and Lord, and your Provider. When you see the Lamb as your Provider, healing comes as Jehovah Rophe is revealed.

This is the key. The moment we see Christ Jesus as provision through redemption, we see healing. The word *provision* is connected to redemption and healing. When Abraham said, *"God will provide himself a lamb"* (Genesis 22:8), he was speaking of redemption. While the sinner may receive healing because of grace, the believer receives healing because of the covenant relationship that comes about through the revelation of who God is.

Abraham and Moses both experienced the revelation of who God is through a revelation of His names, yet there was one great difference between them. Abraham knew the name, but Moses knew what the name could do!

MAY 28–JUNE 3

The Word of God is a word of healing, and the promise of healing is found throughout the Bible.

Benny Hinn

JEHOVAH ROPHE

JUNE

S	M	T	W	T	F	S
28	29	30	31	1	2	3
4	5	6	7	8	9	10
11	12	13	14	15	16	17
18	19	20	21	22	23	24
25	26	27	28	29	30	

My Healer

"Bless the LORD, O my soul, and forget not all his benefits: Who forgiveth all thine iniquities; who healeth all thy diseases."

—Psalm 103:2-3

Healing is not a result of what we do. It is a result of what Christ has already done.

Benny Hinn

JEHOVAH ROPHE

JUNE

S	M	T	W	T	F	S
				1	2	3
4	5	6	7	8	9	10
11	12	13	14	15	16	17
18	19	20	21	22	23	24
25	26	27	28	29	30	

_____

_____

_____

_____

_____

_____

_____

_____

_____

_____

_____

_____

_____

_____

_____

_____

_____

JEHOVAH ROPHE
My Healer

"But he was wounded for our transgressions, he was bruised for our iniquities: the chastisement of our peace was upon him; and with his stripes we are healed."

—Isaiah 53:5

The moment we see Christ Jesus as provision through redemption, we see healing.

Benny Hinn

JUNE

S	M	T	W	T	F	S
				1	2	3
4	5	6	7	8	9	10
11	12	13	14	15	16	17
18	19	20	21	22	23	24
25	26	27	28	29	30	

JEHOVAH ROPHE

_____
_____
_____
_____
_____
_____
_____
_____
_____
_____
_____
_____
_____
_____
_____
_____

JEHOVAH ROPHE
My Healer

"And Jesus went about all Galilee, teaching in their synagogues, and preaching the gospel of the kingdom, and healing all manner of sickness and all manner of disease among the people."

—Matthew 4:23

WEEK OF
JUNE 18–24

God is a healing God, and His presence births the hope of healing, deliverance, and restoration.

Benny Hinn

JEHOVAH ROPHE

JUNE

S	M	T	W	T	F	S
				1	2	3
4	5	6	7	8	9	10
11	12	13	14	15	16	17
18	19	20	21	22	23	24
25	26	27	28	29	30	

_____

_____

_____

_____

_____

_____

_____

_____

_____

_____

_____

_____

_____

_____

_____

_____

_____

_____

JEHOVAH ROPHE
My Healer

"Who his own self bare our sins in his own body on the tree, that we, being dead to sins, should live unto righteousness: by whose stripes ye were healed."

—1 Peter 2:24

Jehovah Nissi

"JEHOVAH NISSI IS WITH
US ON EVERY BATTLEFIELD
OR CHALLENGE, LIFTING
US UP AND LEADING US
TO ULTIMATE VICTORY."

—BENNY HINN

My Banner

JEHOVAH NISSI

Prayer Points:

- Pray for My Father's House children's homes that have been built from the ground up through the support of Benny Hinn Ministries partners and ministry friends. These wonderful facilities include dormitories, administrative buildings, cafeterias, chapels, and vocational training areas where hundreds of children can learn a trade while being nurtured in God's love.

- Lift up the Holy Spirit Miracle Crusade, July 15–17, 2006, in Kobe, Japan, especially for the Lord to anoint the services with His saving and healing power.

- Benny Hinn Ministries and our wonderful partners continue to work with missionaries and local pastors to help start churches around the world. Pray that these efforts will affect coming generations in these strategic areas.

- Join in prayer for a powerful anointing—for God to move mightily during the July 27–28, 2006, Holy Spirit Miracle Crusade at the Fleet Center in Boston.

Jehovah Nissi—"the Lord my Victory" or "the Lord is my Banner"—is used only once in the Word of God (Exodus 17:15). In this memorable passage of Scripture, Amalek's army came to fight with the children of Israel. During the battle, as long as Moses held up the rod, Israel prevailed. When his hands became heavy and he lowered the rod, Amalek prevailed. Finally Aaron and Hur held up his hands as he held up the rod until the battle was won. Afterward, Moses fully recognized that Israel defeated the Amalekites because they were under the Lord's banner: *"Moses built an altar, and called the name of it Jehovahnissi"* (Exodus 17:15).

Nes, the word from which Nissi is derived, refers to a pole with an emblem or crest on it. In battles throughout the centuries, it has been common for warring sides to fly a banner or flag at their front lines to give courage, hope, and a strategic focal point to let the soldiers know how the battle is progressing.

In this revelation of God's name as Jehovah Nissi, we see God's power displayed. He brings victory in defense of His people. God gives us a banner of encouragement. He is with us on every battlefield or challenge, lifting us up, and leading us to ultimate victory.

*God is our banner. He is Jehovah Nissi, the One who wins
our battles and does what we cannot do.*

Benny Hinn

JEHOVAH NISSI

JULY

S	M	T	W	T	F	S
25	26	27	28	29	30	1
2	3	4	5	6	7	8
9	10	11	12	13	14	15
16	17	18	19	20	21	22
23	24	25	26	27	28	29
30	31					

_____

_____

_____

_____

_____

_____

_____

_____

_____

_____

_____

_____

_____

_____

JEHOVAH NISSI
My Banner

"Thine, O LORD, is the greatness, and the power, and the glory, and the victory, and the majesty: for all that is in the heaven and in the earth is thine; thine is the kingdom, O LORD, and thou art exalted as head above all."

—1 Chronicles 29:11

*When you ask God for help, remember that He is faithful—
He gives the victory!*

Benny Hinn

JEHOVAH NISSI

JULY

S	M	T	W	T	F	S
						1
2	3	4	5	6	7	8
9	10	11	12	13	14	15
16	17	18	19	20	21	22
23	24	25	26	27	28	29
30	31					

_____

_____

_____

_____

_____

_____

_____

_____

_____

_____

_____

_____

_____

_____

_____

_____

_____

_____

JEHOVAH NISSI
My Banner

"O sing unto the LORD a new song; for he hath done marvellous things: his right hand, and his holy arm, hath gotten him the victory."

—Psalm 98:1

When you ask God for help, focus on His Word and the victories He has promised.

Benny Hinn

JEHOVAH NISSI

JULY

S	M	T	W	T	F	S
						1
2	3	4	5	6	7	8
9	10	11	12	13	14	15
16	17	18	19	20	21	22
23	24	25	26	27	28	29
30	31					

_____

_____

_____

_____

_____

_____

_____

_____

_____

_____

_____

_____

_____

_____

_____

_____

_____

_____

JEHOVAH NISSI
My Banner

"But thanks be to God, which giveth us the victory through our Lord Jesus Christ."

—1 Corinthians 15:57

Jehovah Nissi is greater than all the forces of the world. He provides victory as we overcome all challenges through God's Word.

Benny Hinn

JEHOVAH NISSI

JULY

S	M	T	W	T	F	S
						1
2	3	4	5	6	7	8
9	10	11	12	13	14	15
16	17	18	19	20	21	22
23	24	25	26	27	28	29
30	31					

_____

_____

_____

_____

_____

_____

_____

_____

_____

_____

_____

_____

_____

_____

_____

_____

_____

_____

_____

JEHOVAH NISSI
My Banner

"Ye are of God, little children, and have overcome them: because greater is he that is in you, than he that is in the world."

—1 John 4:4

Keep your eyes on God, and thank Him for the victory!

Benny Hinn

JEHOVAH NISSI

JULY

S	M	T	W	T	F	S
						1
2	3	4	5	6	7	8
9	10	11	12	13	14	15
16	17	18	19	20	21	22
23	24	25	26	27	28	29
30	31					

My Banner

"For whatsoever is born of God overcometh the world: and this is the victory that overcometh the world, even our faith."

—1 John 5:4

Jehovah Mikkadesh

"THROUGHOUT THE BIBLE, GOD CALLS US TO BE SANCTIFIED, OR SET APART."

—BENNY HINN

My Sanctifier

Jehovah Mikkadesh, ***Jehovah M'Kaddesh***—"the Lord my Sanctifier"—makes us whole and sets us apart to be holy. *Mikkadesh* comes from the Hebrew word *qâdash,* which means "sanctify," "holy," or "dedicate."

It is recorded in the Scriptures: *"And the LORD spake unto Moses, saying, Speak thou also unto the children of Israel, saying, Verily my sabbaths ye shall keep: for it is a sign between me and you throughout your generations; that ye may know that I am the LORD that doth sanctify you"* (Exodus 31:12-13).

The next glorious revelation of God's name is found in Leviticus 20:7-8: *"Sanctify yourselves therefore, and be ye holy: for I am the LORD your God. And ye shall keep my statutes, and do them: I am the LORD which sanctify you."*

Throughout the Bible, God calls us to be sanctified, or set apart. In Genesis, for example, God reveals sin. In Exodus He reveals redemption. And in Leviticus He reveals sanctification. As you and I choose to follow God's example of holiness, we become more like Him. Sanctification sets us apart for service.

Prayer Points:

- Pray that God's power will continue to touch millions of lives each year through Pastor Benny's life-changing teachings which are distributed through books, videos, CDs, and DVDs.

- Agree in prayer that God will prepare the hearts of those who attend the August 25–26, 2006, Holy Spirit Miracle Crusade in London, and that those whose lives are changed will become part of strong churches as the outpouring moves upon the UK, Europe, and beyond.

- Lift up the ministers of the World Healing Fellowship, especially during the exciting Pastors Conference during August 30–September 1, 2006, in Grapevine, Texas. The Fellowship serves people with cutting-edge technologies, scripturally sound resources, and biblically based encouragement.

- Pray for Benny Hinn Ministries' church plantings. Many are in remote villages in Middle Eastern countries that are more open to the Gospel than ever before. Entire regions are receiving the saving, healing message of God's Word through these outreaches because of our partners and friends.

JEHOVAH MIKKADESH

JEHOVAH MIKKADESH

AUGUST

S	M	T	W	T	F	S
30	31	1	2	3	4	5
6	7	8	9	10	11	12
13	14	15	16	17	18	19
20	21	22	23	24	25	26
27	28	29	30	31		

True sanctification not only is absolutely essential and unspeakably precious, it is impossible to attain by yourself. It is supernatural, revealed by God through His Holy Word.

Benny Hinn

JEHOVAH MIKKADESH

My Sanctifier

"They shall therefore keep mine ordinance...I the LORD do sanctify them."

—Leviticus 22:9

AUGUST 6–12

Sanctification means to be set apart by God for a holy and special use.

Benny Hinn

JEHOVAH MIKKADESH

AUGUST

S	M	T	W	T	F	S
		1	2	3	4	5
6	7	8	9	10	11	12
13	14	15	16	17	18	19
20	21	22	23	24	25	26
27	28	29	30	31		

_____

_____

_____

_____

_____

_____

_____

_____

_____

_____

_____

_____

_____

_____

_____

_____

_____

_____

JEHOVAH MIKKADESH

My Sanctifier

"For I am the LORD your God: ye shall therefore sanctify yourselves, and ye shall be holy; for I am holy."

—Leviticus 11:44

Sanctification sets us apart for service.

Benny Hinn

JEHOVAH MIKKADESH

AUGUST

S	M	T	W	T	F	S
		1	2	3	4	5
6	7	8	9	10	11	12
13	14	15	16	17	18	19
20	21	22	23	24	25	26
27	28	29	30	31		

_____

_____

_____

_____

_____

_____

_____

_____

_____

_____

_____

_____

_____

JEHOVAH MIKKADESH
My Sanctifier

"Therefore shall ye keep my commandments, and do them: I am the LORD. Neither shall ye profane my holy name...I am the LORD which hallow you, That brought you out of the land of Egypt, to be your God: I am the LORD."

—Leviticus 22:31-33

As we choose to follow our Lord's example of holiness, we become more like Him.

Benny Hinn

AUGUST

S	M	T	W	T	F	S
		1	2	3	4	5
6	7	8	9	10	11	12
13	14	15	16	17	18	19
20	21	22	23	24	25	26
27	28	29	30	31		

JEHOVAH MIKKADESH

_____

_____

_____

_____

_____

_____

_____

_____

_____

_____

_____

JEHOVAH MIKKADESH

My Sanctifier

"These words spake Jesus, and lifted up his eyes to heaven, and said.... Sanctify them through thy truth: thy word is truth. As thou hast sent me into the world, even so have I also sent them into the world. And for their sakes I sanctify myself, that they also might be sanctified through the truth."

—John 17:1, 17-19

Jehovah Tsidkenu

"RIGHTEOUSNESS IS
IMPOSSIBLE WITHOUT
GOD, FOR THE LORD IS
OUR RIGHTEOUSNESS."

—BENNY HINN

My Righteousness

Jehovah Tsidkenu—first used in Jeremiah 23:5-6 then again in Jeremiah 33:16—is filled with meaning. *Tsedek*, from which *Tsidkenu* is derived, means "to be stiff," "to be straight," or "righteous."

When the two words are combined, Jehovah Tsidkenu, we have "the LORD who is our Righteousness." This refers to justice. It means being allowed to be in a right relationship with God because of His righteousness, for He becomes our righteousness as we accept His Son Jesus as our Lord and Savior:

> *Behold, the days come, saith the LORD, that I will raise unto David a righteous Branch, and a King shall reign and prosper, and shall execute judgment and justice in the earth. In his days Judah shall be saved, and Israel shall dwell safely: and this is his name whereby he shall be called, THE LORD OUR RIGHTEOUSNESS.* (Jeremiah 23:5-6)

In this revelation, we recognize that righteousness is impossible without God. The Lord is our righteousness, *"for he hath made him to be sin for us, who knew no sin; that we might be made the righteousness of God in him"* (2 Corinthians 5:21). Jehovah Tsidkenu is our righteousness!

Prayer Points:

- Pray that God will use our disaster relief outreach programs ongoing throughout the world. These efforts, in cooperation with partnerships in each region, made available through the generosity of ministry friends, are invaluable in opening doors to spread the Gospel.

- Lift up the youth service on September 9, 2006, in Tulsa. Pastor Benny's desire to reach youth continues to expand through explosive youth services filling the largest arenas. Pray for God's power to be poured out on young people, who in turn can help reach the world for the Savior.

- Pray for doors to open for Pastor Benny, as he is often sought after for prayer and personal ministry by people in the highest levels of church, government, business, and entertainment. He is often asked to address parliaments and governing bodies where he holds crusades.

- Pray for God's power to be poured out in Greece at the September 22–23 Holy Spirit Miracle Crusade in Athens.

JEHOVAH TSIDKENU

AUGUST 27–SEPTEMBER 2

God's righteousness provides security and peace, even in the storms of life.

Benny Hinn

SEPTEMBER

S	M	T	W	T	F	S
27	28	29	30	31	1	2
3	4	5	6	7	8	9
10	11	12	13	14	15	16
17	18	19	20	21	22	23
24	25	26	27	28	29	30

JEHOVAH TSIDKENU

_____

_____

_____

_____

_____

_____

_____

_____

_____

_____

_____

_____

_____

_____

_____

_____

_____

JEHOVAH TSIDKENU

My Righteousness

"He restoreth my soul: he leadeth me in the paths of righteousness for his name's sake."

—Psalm 23:3

The righteousness, available to you through the death of Jesus Christ, offers you legal acceptance and approval before God.

Benny Hinn

JEHOVAH TSIDKENU

SEPTEMBER

S	M	T	W	T	F	S
					1	2
3	4	5	6	7	8	9
10	11	12	13	14	15	16
17	18	19	20	21	22	23
24	25	26	27	28	29	30

JEHOVAH TSIDKENU

My Righteousness

"In those days shall Judah be saved, and Jerusalem shall dwell safely: and this is the name wherewith she shall be called, The LORD our righteousness."

—Jeremiah 33:16

Belonging to God is not just a religion—it is a relationship and a fellowship made possible only through the righteousness purchased through the blood of Jesus Christ.

Benny Hinn

SEPTEMBER

S	M	T	W	T	F	S
					1	2
3	4	5	6	7	8	9
10	11	12	13	14	15	16
17	18	19	20	21	22	23
24	25	26	27	28	29	30

JEHOVAH TSIDKENU

_____

_____

_____

_____

_____

_____

_____

_____

_____

_____

_____

_____

_____

_____

_____

_____

_____

JEHOVAH TSIDKENU

My Righteousness

"Thy righteousness also, O God, is very high, who hast done great things: O God, who is like unto thee!"

—Psalm 71:19

Jesus Christ came to die on the cross for your sins. He became your perfect righteousness..

Benny Hinn

SEPTEMBER

S	M	T	W	T	F	S
					1	2
3	4	5	6	7	8	9
10	11	12	13	14	15	16
17	18	19	20	21	22	23
24	25	26	27	28	29	30

JEHOVAH TSIDKENU

_____

_____

_____

_____

_____

_____

_____

_____

_____

_____

_____

_____

_____

_____

_____

_____

JEHOVAH TSIDKENU

My Righteousness

"But the mercy of the LORD is from everlasting to everlasting upon them that fear him, and his righteousness unto children's children."

—Psalm 103:17

Those who belong to Jesus Christ, because of the righteousness He provides, can enjoy a close relationship with God on earth and look forward to an eternal inheritance in heaven.

Benny Hinn

JEHOVAH TSIDKENU

SEPTEMBER

S	M	T	W	T	F	S
					1	2
3	4	5	6	7	8	9
10	11	12	13	14	15	16
17	18	19	20	21	22	23
24	25	26	27	28	29	30

_____

_____

_____

_____

_____

_____

_____

_____

_____

_____

_____

_____

_____

_____

_____

_____

JEHOVAH TSIDKENU
My Righteousness

"Fear thou not; for I am with thee: be not dismayed; for I am thy God: I will strengthen thee; yea, I will help thee; yea, I will uphold thee with the right hand of my righteousness."

—Isaiah 41:10

Jehovah Shalom

"THE PEACE THAT
STILLED GIDEON'S
TROUBLED HEART
WAS SUPERNATU-
RALLY GIVEN BY
THE LORD. THIS
IS A PEACE MADE
POSSIBLE ONLY BY
COMING TO KNOW
GOD AS JEHOVAH
SHALOM."

—BENNY HINN

My Peace

J E H O V A H   S H A L O M

Prayer Points:

- Join in prayer for a special anointing of God's saving and healing power during the Holy Spirit Miracle Crusade, October 12–13, 2006, in San Antonio, Texas.

- Pray for the Calcutta Mercy Hospital in India. Located in a city of 11 million people and surrounded by a country with a population now topping a billion, this facility—completely underwritten by the partners of Benny Hinn Ministries—is an open door to reaching this country with the Gospel.

- Intercede with worldwide prayer warriors for a powerful outpouring during the Holy Spirit Miracle Crusade to be held October 27–29 in Buenos Aries, Argentina, at the River Plate Stadium.

- Agree in prayer for Benny Hinn Ministries Spanish-language telecasts to continue to expand throughout the Americas. Also, pray for our 24-hour-a-day Arabic-language satellite network that blankets the Middle East, Europe, and North Africa with teaching, preaching, and original dramatic programs.

Jehovah Shalom—"the Lord my Peace" or "the Lord is Peace"—is used 170 times in the Old Testament. It was revealed to Gideon after the Lord called and commanded him to smite the Midianites: *"Then Gideon built an altar there unto the LORD, and called it Jehovahshalom"* (Judges 6:24).

Despite their miraculous liberation from Egypt, the Israelites soon forgot that the Lord had rescued them from bondage. Forced to wander in the wilderness, the Israelites found themselves confronted by the Midianites, who, lacking sufficient manpower to wage war on their own, often formed coalitions with other local people to become a formidable foe.

In commanding Gideon to lead the Israelites into battle against the Midianites, God assured him: *"Surely I will be with thee, and thou shalt smite the Midianites as one man"* (Judges 6:16). Gideon, though, was unaware of who he was in God and disclosed the unbelief in his heart, saying, *"If now I have found grace in thy sight, then shew me a sign"* (Judges 6:17).

God then revealed Himself to Gideon, whose fear and unbelief vanished, leaving his life filled with peace through obedience to God. Following God's revelation of Himself to Gideon as Jehovah Shalom, Gideon led 300 men to a supernatural victory over the Midianites.

True peace is made possible only by coming to know God as Jehovah Shalom.

The peace that stills troubled hearts—even in the midst of battle—is supernaturally given by Jehovah Shalom.

Benny Hinn

OCTOBER

S	M	T	W	T	F	S
1	2	3	4	5	6	7
8	9	10	11	12	13	14
15	16	17	18	19	20	21
22	23	24	25	26	27	28
29	30	31				

JEHOVAH SHALOM

_____

_____

_____

_____

_____

_____

_____

_____

_____

_____

_____

_____

JEHOVAH SHALOM

My Peace

"As for me, I will call upon God; and the LORD shall save me. Evening, and morning, and at noon, will I pray, and cry aloud: and he shall hear my voice. He hath delivered my soul in peace from the battle that was against me."

—Psalm 55:16-18

Where Jehovah Shalom is known and worshiped, peace reigns.

Benny Hinn

OCTOBER

S	M	T	W	T	F	S
1	2	3	4	5	6	7
8	9	10	11	12	13	14
15	16	17	18	19	20	21
22	23	24	25	26	27	28
29	30	31				

JEHOVAH SHALOM

JEHOVAH SHALOM

My Peace

"And let the peace of God rule in your hearts."

—Colossians 3:15

God's peace is beyond human knowledge and understanding.

Benny Hinn

OCTOBER

S	M	T	W	T	F	S
1	2	3	4	5	6	7
8	9	10	11	12	13	14
15	16	17	18	19	20	21
22	23	24	25	26	27	28
29	30	31				

JEHOVAH SHALOM

_____

_____

_____

_____

_____

_____

_____

_____

_____

_____

_____

_____

_____

_____

_____

JEHOVAH SHALOM

My Peace

"Peace I leave with you, my peace I give unto you: not as the world giveth, give I unto you. Let not your heart be troubled, neither let it be afraid."

—John 14:27

Where the Prince of Peace reigns, peace reigns.

Benny Hinn

JEHOVAH SHALOM

OCTOBER

S	M	T	W	T	F	S
1	2	3	4	5	6	7
8	9	10	11	12	13	14
15	16	17	18	19	20	21
22	23	24	25	26	27	28
29	30	31				

JEHOVAH SHALOM

My Peace

"And the peace of God, which passeth all understanding, shall keep your hearts and minds through Christ Jesus."

—Philippians 4:7

Jehovah Rohi

"No other
revelation of
God's name
conveys such
tender intimacy
and fellowship
as Jehovah
Rohi."

—Benny Hinn

My Shepherd

JEHOVAH ROHI

Jehovah Rohi, Jehovah Ro'eh—"my Shepherd"—occurs in Genesis 48:15; 49:24, and Psalm 23:1; 80:1. The root word for *Rohi* means "shepherd," and it also means "intimate friendship" or "close companionship."

In Psalm 23, one of the most familiar of all Bible passages, David wrote under the inspiration of the Holy Spirit these memorable words: *"The LORD is my shepherd, I shall not want"* (verse 1). With these words, the youthful shepherd spoke of the bond of intimacy the Lord desires to have with His people, as a Shepherd who guides His sheep, protecting and nurturing them.

Even to eternity, God promises unspeakable blessings for those who follow the Lamb of God—Jesus, our Shepherd:

> *And one of the elders answered, saying unto me, What are these which are arrayed in white robes? and whence came they? And I said unto him, Sir, thou knowest. And he said to me, These are they which came out of great tribulation, and have washed their robes, and made them white in the blood of the Lamb. Therefore are they before the throne of God, and serve him day and night in his temple: and he that sitteth on the throne shall dwell among them. They shall hunger no more, neither thirst any more; neither shall the sun light on them, nor any heat. For the Lamb which is in the midst of the throne shall feed them, and shall lead them unto living fountains of waters: and God shall wipe away all tears from their eyes.* (Revelation 7:13-17)

No other revelation of God's name conveys such tender intimacy and fellowship as Jehovah Rohi.

How tenderly Jehovah Rohi cherishes His sheep!

Benny Hinn

JEHOVAH ROHI

NOVEMBER

S	M	T	W	T	F	S
29	30	31	1	2	3	4
5	6	7	8	9	10	11
12	13	14	15	16	17	18
19	20	21	22	23	24	25
26	27	28	29	30		

_____

_____

_____

_____

_____

_____

_____

_____

_____

_____

_____

_____

_____

JEHOVAH ROHI

My Shepherd

"Behold, the Lord GOD will come with strong hand, and his arm shall rule for him: behold, his reward is with him, and his work before him. He shall feed his flock like a shepherd: he shall gather the lambs with his arm, and carry them in his bosom, and shall gently lead those that are with young."

—Isaiah 40:10-11

Even when one sheep goes astray, a caring shepherd goes after it and restores it to the flock. So it is with Jesus Christ, the Good Shepherd.

Benny Hinn

NOVEMBER

S	M	T	W	T	F	S
			1	2	3	4
5	6	7	8	9	10	11
12	13	14	15	16	17	18
19	20	21	22	23	24	25
26	27	28	29	30		

JEHOVAH ROHI

_____

_____

_____

_____

_____

_____

_____

_____

_____

_____

_____

JEHOVAH ROHI
My Shepherd

"What man of you, having an hundred sheep, if he lose one of them, doth not leave the ninety and nine in the wilderness, and go after that which is lost, until he find it? And when he hath found it, he layeth it on his shoulders, rejoicing. And when he cometh home, he calleth together his friends and neighbours, saying unto them, Rejoice with me; for I have found my sheep which was lost."

—Luke 15:4-6

Jesus is the Good Shepherd, for His sacrifice on the cross bought salvation for anyone who believes in Him.

Benny Hinn

JEHOVAH ROHI

NOVEMBER

S	M	T	W	T	F	S
			1	2	3	4
5	6	7	8	9	10	11
12	13	14	15	16	17	18
19	20	21	22	23	24	25
26	27	28	29	30		

My Shepherd

"As the Father knoweth me, even so know I the Father: and I lay down my life for the sheep."

—John 10:15

As sheep in the field respond to their shepherd's voice, so must we also continually listen to our Lord's instructions.

Benny Hinn

NOVEMBER

S	M	T	W	T	F	S
			1	2	3	4
5	6	7	8	9	10	11
12	13	14	15	16	17	18
19	20	21	22	23	24	25
26	27	28	29	30		

JEHOVAH ROHI

JEHOVAH ROHI

My Shepherd

"My sheep hear my voice, and I know them, and they follow me."

—John 10:27

Jehovah Shammah

"When God is present in our lives, He leads us into the grandeur and the glory of His abiding presence, for we know we shall dwell with Jehovah Shammah forever!"

—Benny Hinn

My Abiding Presence

JEHOVAH SHAMMAH

Prayer Points:

- Pray in agreement for God's protection, guidance, and anointing as Pastor Benny and the ministry team goes to Hyderabad, India, for the massive Festival of Blessings.

- Intercede for the television programs produced by Benny Hinn Ministries: *This Is Your Day!* which premiered in 1990 and is one of the most-watched Christian telecasts around the world, and *Manna from Heaven*, featuring Pastor Benny's in-depth teaching of God's Word.

- Lift up the dedicated staff of the Calcutta Mercy Hospital in Calcutta, India. Benny Hinn Ministries partners completely underwrites all expenses of the hospital, where over 200,000 patients are treated each year.

- Even as we celebrate the joyous season of the birth of our Lord Jesus, be in prayer for upcoming 2007 Holy Spirit Miracle Crusades throughout the world, that God would continue to open amazing doors of opportunity to the preaching of the Gospel.

Jehovah Shammah—"His Abiding Presence" or "the Lord is there"—is used only once in the Bible, in Ezekiel 48:35, the last verse of Ezekiel's prophetic book. This glorious revelation deals with the abiding presence of God. *Shammah* is derived from the Hebrew word *sham*, which can be translated as "there," spoken of by Ezekiel the prophet after he was shown the millennium temple and the glory of God.

As a twenty-five-year-old exile in Babylon, Ezekiel prophesied the destruction of Jerusalem eleven years before judgment fell on that city. Years later, and still residing among the Babylonians, Ezekiel began to prophesy the restoration of God's glory. He described a temple and a city of the future in which the glory of God shall abide forever, declaring, *"And the name of the city from that day shall be, The LORD is there"* (Ezekiel 48:35).

When God is present in our lives, He leads us into the grandeur and the glory of His abiding presence, for we know we shall dwell with Jehovah Shammah forever!

WEEK OF
NOVEMBER 26–DECEMBER 2

God seeks fellowship, abiding fellowship, with His children and those who abide in Him receive supernatural protection.

Benny Hinn

JEHOVAH SHAMMAH

DECEMBER

S	M	T	W	T	F	S
26	27	28	29	30	1	2
3	4	5	6	7	8	9
10	11	12	13	14	15	16
17	18	19	20	21	22	23
24	25	26	27	28	29	30
31						

_____

_____

_____

_____

_____

_____

_____

_____

_____

_____

_____

_____

_____

_____

_____

_____

_____

_____

JEHOVAH SHAMMAH

My Abiding Presence

"He that dwelleth in the secret place of the most High shall abide under the shadow of the Almighty."

—Psalm 91:1

God abides among those who seek Him for refuge and safety.

Benny Hinn

JEHOVAH SHAMMAH

DECEMBER

S	M	T	W	T	F	S
					1	2
3	4	5	6	7	8	9
10	11	12	13	14	15	16
17	18	19	20	21	22	23
24	25	26	27	28	29	30
31						

_____

_____

_____

_____

_____

_____

_____

_____

_____

_____

_____

_____

_____

_____

JEHOVAH SHAMMAH

My Abiding Presence

"The LORD thy God in the midst of thee is mighty; he will save, he will rejoice over thee with joy."

—Zephaniah 3:17

God places His glory among the body of believers, even as He provides protection from the enemy of our souls.

Benny Hinn

JEHOVAH SHAMMAH

DECEMBER

S	M	T	W	T	F	S
					1	2
3	4	5	6	7	8	9
10	11	12	13	14	15	16
17	18	19	20	21	22	23
24	25	26	27	28	29	30
31						

_____
_____
_____
_____
_____
_____
_____
_____
_____
_____
_____
_____
_____
_____
_____
_____
_____
_____

JEHOVAH SHAMMAH

My Abiding Presence

"I...will be unto her a wall of fire round about, and will be the glory in the midst of her."

—Zechariah 2:5

God's Word brings His abiding presence into our lives. His abiding presence fulfills all our needs.

Benny Hinn

JEHOVAH SHAMMAH

DECEMBER

S	M	T	W	T	F	S
					1	2
3	4	5	6	7	8	9
10	11	12	13	14	15	16
17	18	19	20	21	22	23
24	25	26	27	28	29	30
31						

_____

_____

_____

_____

_____

_____

_____

_____

_____

_____

_____

_____

_____

_____

_____

_____

_____

JEHOVAH SHAMMAH

My Abiding Presence

"If ye abide in me, and my words abide in you, ye shall ask what ye will, and it shall be done unto you."

—John 15:7

Jehovah Shammah's abiding presence gives boldness and purpose today. More importantly, His presence gives glorious hope for tomorrow!

Benny Hinn

JEHOVAH SHAMMAH

DECEMBER

S	M	T	W	T	F	S
					1	2
3	4	5	6	7	8	9
10	11	12	13	14	15	16
17	18	19	20	21	22	23
24	25	26	27	28	29	30
31						

_____

_____

_____

_____

_____

_____

_____

_____

_____

_____

_____

_____

_____

_____

_____

_____

_____

JEHOVAH SHAMMAH

My Abiding Presence

"And now, little children, abide in him; that, when he shall appear, we
may have confidence, and not be ashamed before him at his coming."

—1 John 2:28

As you dwell in the presence of Jehovah Shammah during 2007, you can know without a shadow of doubt that "the Lord is there" every day of the coming year. Understanding that truth will transform your life both now and evermore!

JEHOVAH SHAMMAH

DECEMBER

S	M	T	W	T	F	S
					1	2
3	4	5	6	7	8	9
10	11	12	13	14	15	16
17	18	19	20	21	22	23
24	25	26	27	28	29	30
31						

_____

_____

_____

_____

_____

_____

_____

_____

_____

_____

_____

_____

_____

_____

JEHOVAH SHAMMAH

My Abiding Presence

"Now unto him that is able to keep you from falling, and to present you faultless before the presence of his glory with exceeding joy. To the only wise God our Saviour, be glory and majesty, dominion and power, both now and ever. Amen."

—Jude 24-25

THE 12
NAMES OF GOD
PRAYER JOURNAL

2006

_____

_____

_____

_____

_____

_____

_____

_____

_____

_____

_____

_____

_____

_____

_____

_____

_____

_____

_____

_____

_____

_____

_____

_____